Test Your Vocabulary – Book 3

Peter Watcyn-Jones

Illustrated by Sven Nordqvist

PENGUIN BOOKS

PENGUIN BOOKS

Published by the Penguin Group
27 Wrights Lane, London W8 5TZ, England
Viking Penguin Inc., 40 West 23rd Street, New York, New York 10010, USA
Penguin Books Australia Ltd, Ringwood, Victoria, Australia
Penguin Books Canada Ltd, 2801 John Street, Markham, Ontario, Canada L3R 1B4
Penguin Books (NZ) Ltd, 182–190 Wairau Road, Auckland 10, New Zealand

Penguin Books Ltd, Registered Offices: Harmondsworth, Middlesex, England

First published in Sweden by Kursverksamhetens förlag 1982
Published in Penguin Books 1985
10 9 8 7 6

Made and printed in Great Britain by
Hazell Watson & Viney Limited
Member of BPCC plc
Aylesbury, Bucks, England
Set in Times

INTRODUCTION

Owing to the emphasis in recent years on functional and communicative approaches to language learning, many other important areas of the language have been neglected. One such area is vocabulary. This series is an attempt to remedy this situation not only by filling a real gap in the materials available but also by attempting to show that vocabulary learning can be just as much fun and just as stimulating as other activities. There are five books altogether in the series, ranging from Elementary level to Advanced. Each book contains fifty tests or exercises and, to facilitate self-study, a key is also included. Students using these books should find vocabulary learning both stimulating and enjoyable and, hopefully, start to develop a real sensitivity to the language.

Test Your Vocabulary – Book 3 is the fourth book in the series and is intended for intermediate/advanced students. There are approximately 700 words in the book and although the tests are similar in layout and areas of vocabulary to the previous two books, important additions are tests based on word-building and phrasal verbs. Again there are a number of picture tests plus tests which concentrate on words and prepositions which pose particular problems for foreign learners. This book is particularly useful for students studying for the Cambridge First Certificate examination or similar examinations where there is a heavy emphasis on lexis.

TO THE STUDENT

This book will help you to learn a lot of new English words. But in order for the new words to become "fixed" in your mind, you need to test yourself again and again. Here is one method you can use to help you learn the words:

1. Read through the instructions carefully for the test you are going to try. Then try the test, writing your answers **in pencil**.
2. When you have finished, check your answers and correct any mistakes you have made. Read through the test again, paying special attention to the words you didn't know or got wrong.
3. Try the test again five minutes later. You can do this either by covering up the words (for example, in the picture tests) or by asking a friend to test you. Repeat this until you can remember all the words.
4. **Rub out your answers**.
5. Try the test again the following day. (You should remember most of the words.)
6. Finally, plan to try the test at least twice again within the following month. After this most of the words will be "fixed" in your mind.

CONTENTS

1 Receptacles – containers

Write the number of each drawing next to the correct word or words.

goblet	. . . . .
tea caddy	. . . . .
barrel	. . . . .
bread bin	. . . . .
crate	. . . . .
filing cabinet	. . . . .
carrier bag	. . . . .
sheath	. . . . .
satchel	. . . . .
cage	. . . . .
rucksack	. . . . .
keg	. . . . .
wastepaper basket	. . . . .
litterbin	. . . . .
trunk	. . . . .

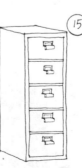

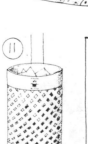

2 Phrases

Look at the following drawings, then fill in the missing words. Choose from the questions/statements (1–12) and the responses (a–l) below.

1 Excuse me, is anyone sitting here?
2 I didn't know John was married.
3 I'm sorry I'm late.
4 Thanks for the flowers, Jim.
5 My father's much better now.

6 Have you got a light, please?
7 Pass the salt, please.
8 Do you mind if I switch the light off?
9 If only I hadn't said that to her.
10 You couldn't give me a hand, could you?
11 My mother's just had her first novel accepted.
12 May I come in?

a It's a pleasure.
b Has she really? How wonderful!
c No, of course not.
d Certainly. Here you are.
e Well, I'd rather you didn't, darling, if you don't mind.
f No, neither did I.
g Yes, please do.
h Oh, that's all right.
i Yes, of course.
j Sorry, I don't smoke.

k Ah well! That's life!

l Oh, I'm so pleased to hear it.

3 Tools, etc.

Write the number of each drawing next to the correct word or words.

hatchet	. . . . .
callipers	. . . . .
mallet	. . . . .
spirit level	. . . . .
hoe	. . . . .
tape measure	. . . . .
pickaxe	. . . . .
oilcan	. . . . .
trowel	. . . . .
hacksaw	. . . . .
awl	. . . . .
fork	. . . . .

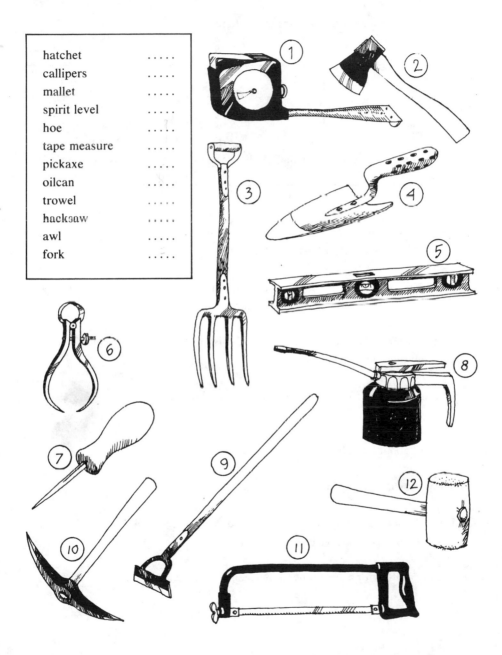

4 Missing words – Newspapers and television

Put the following words into the correct sentences:

journalist	chat show	cartoon strip	classified
cartoonist	headline	review	channels
serial	dubbed	documentary	leader
series	quiz	article	action replay
editor	circulation	caption	gossip column

1 There was a huge .... on the front page this morning. It said "PEACE IN THE MIDDLE EAST".

2 It certainly looked like a penalty, but when they showed the .... of it you could see quite clearly that he hadn't been fouled.

3 A story which is divided into a number of episodes, each one beginning where the previous one ended, is called a ....

4 The number of copies a newspaper sells every day is called its ....

5 A report about a new book, play or film is called a ....

6 The person in charge of a newspaper is called the ....

7 If you are looking for a flat or a car then you can always look at the .... advertisements in a newspaper.

8 A story written for a newspaper or magazine is called an ....

9 In many countries foreign television programmes are .... to enable viewers to understand what is being said.

10 Someone who writes for a newspaper is called a ....

11 In Britain, there are four television .... — BBC 1, BBC 2, ITV, and Channel 4.

12 There was a fantastic .... on TV last night about the life of Eskimos.

13 A programme in which an interviewer talks to a number of well-known personalities is called a ....

14 "The Brothers" was perhaps one of the best television .... ever made.

15 The words under a cartoon are called the ....

16 You read the .... to find out what the newspaper thought about the latest news.

17 A series of drawings in a newspaper every day about characters such as The Gambols, Andy Capp, Charlie Brown, etc. is called a ....

18 A person who draws these is called a ....

19 A television programme where people compete against one another by answering questions is called a .... programme.

20 In many newspapers there is a special page with news about well-known people in society (e.g. writers, film stars, members of the Royal Family, etc) — especially if they have new boyfriends, girlfriends or are involved in some sort of scandal. This page is called the ....

5 Word building 1

The word in capitals at the end of each of the following sentences can be used to form a word that fits suitably in the blank space. Fill in each blank this way.

Example: During the War, there was a great ..*SHORTAGE*..   SHORT
            of sugar, coffee and other goods.

1 My uncle's got a very interesting ....   OCCUPY
   He's a television announcer.

2 I don't think guns are .... toys for   SUIT
   young children.

3 I sometimes wonder whether the world would not have   INVENT
   been a better place without the ....
   of television.

4 It is almost .... for young people   POSSIBLE
   leaving school today to get a job.

5 Many people still refuse to believe that smoking is   HARM
   ....

6 Björn Borg is probably the most ....   SUCCESS
   tennis player of all time.

7 I was kept .... last night by the   WAKE
   noise from a party in the flat above.

8 Elizabeth Taylor won an Oscar for her ....   PERFORM
   in "Who's afraid of Virginia Woolf?"

9 Many people think it is very ....   DOUBT
   whether a cure will be found for cancer before the year
   2000.

10 My wife is .... of spiders.   TERROR

11 Although the painting looked like a genuine Picasso, the   SIGN
   .... was definitely a fake.

12 When I.B.M. advertised for a new Production Manager,   APPLY
   they received over fifty .... for
   the job.

13 He's so nice. It's a .... working for   PLEASE
   him.

14 You shouldn't have mentioned death. You know how .... Charles is about that sort of thing. SENSE

15 It is becoming .... difficult to find a job nowadays. INCREASE

16 I understand your problem, Miss Brown, and don't think I'm not ...., but we really can't allow you to phone up your boyfriend in America using the office phone. SYMPATHY

17 Nowadays, violence seems to be a .... occurrence. DAY

18 While money can't exactly buy you .... at least it helps you suffer in comfort. HAPPY

19 John's a nice person – he's kind, generous, sympathetic. But I couldn't go out with him – he's just so .... to look at. ATTRACT

20 But how could you do it? Really, Ophelia, I feel quite .... of you! SHAME

6 Definitions 1 – Types of people

Fill in the missing words in the definitions below. Choose from the following:

bitchy	gregarious	conceited
bossy	impulsive	absent-minded
timid	garrulous	tetchy
punctual	witty	industrious
bigoted	reliable	stoical

1 A/an .... person is someone who is easily frightened and is not very brave.

2 A/an .... person is someone who habitually talks too much – especially about things which are not very important.

3 A/an .... person is someone you can trust and depend on at all times.

4 A/an .... person is someone who is so concerned with his or her thoughts that he or she doesn't notice what is happening or what he or she is doing and, as a result, often forgets things.

5 A/an .... person is someone who is hard-working.

6 A/an .... person is someone who is sensitive in a bad-tempered sort of way.

7 A/an .... person is someone who enjoys giving other people orders.

8 A/an .... person is someone who never shows dislike, worry, etc. when faced with something unpleasant, but who always remains calm.

9 A/an .... person is someone who has a tendency to make nasty jokes about other people and who finds fault with everything.

10 A/an .... person is someone who is very sociable and enjoys the company of other people.

11 A/an .... person is someone who is never late, but who always arrives at the exact or agreed time.

12 A/an .... person is someone who believes strongly and often unreasonably that he or she is right and best (especially in matters of religion, race or politics).

13 A/an .... person is someone who is able to make clever, amusing remarks.

14 A/an .... person is someone who has a tendency to do something without thinking about the results or consequences of his or her actions beforehand.

15 A/an .... person is someone who has a very high opinion of himself or herself – especially about his or her abilities, etc.

7 Too many words

Replace the words in bold type in the following sentences with a single word. (The first letter of the word is given.)

1 The **man who controls a tennis match** told Connors to start serving. (u ....
    ....)
2 He **was very sorry for** the way he had behaved. (r................................)
3 Many people **told beforehand** that John F. Kennedy would be assassinated.
    (f................................)
4 He was a happy person who was always **expecting the best to happen.** (o..............
    ....)
5 Last weekend I had the horrible experience of having to visit the **place where
    dead bodies are kept until the funeral.** (m................................)
6 Because of the bad acoustics, the actor's words were **so low that they could not be
    heard.** (i................................)
7 The **people who were sitting in the church** listened attentively to the vicar's
    sermon. (c................................)
8 He had great **strength of body to fight tiredness** and could run for hours without
    stopping. (s................................)
9 My cousin is **able to use both hands equally well.** This was a great advantage when
    he broke his arm since he could still write with his other hand. (a......................)
10 My doctor gave me sleeping pills because I was suffering from **a prolonged in-
    ability to sleep.** (i................................)
11 I've just bought a cottage on an island in the **group of islands** outside Stock-
    holm. (a................................)
12 I've just read a very good **written account of the life** of Beethoven. (b.................)
13 The student **said he was sorry** for his bad behaviour. (a................................)
14 As a child I always wanted to be a **person who performs operations at a hospital.**
    (s................................)
15 I must have drunk too much at the party last night. I woke up this morning with a
    terrible **headache and a feeling of wanting to be sick.** (h................................)
16 As I was reversing into the garage I ran into a post and badly dented the **metal
    bar fixed at the back of a car for protection.** (b................................)

17 Which **room for patients at the hospital** is your mother in? (w............................)

18 I know it looks difficult at the moment, but don't worry – things will work out **in one way or another**. (s................................)

19 Two cars **drove into one another** at a crossroads this morning in the village of Ninfield, but fortunately no one was hurt. (c................................)

20 By the way, this is my **brother's son**, Roger. (n................................)

8 Choose the word 1

Choose the word which best completes each sentence.

1 Before the sermon, the vicar asked the .... to sit down.
   a audience   b assembly   c crowd   d congregation
   e constituents

2 After hours of wandering around in the desert they thought they saw an oasis,
   but they were wrong. There was nothing there; it was only a ....
   a ghost   b mirage   c trick   d vision
   e mirror

3 The boxer hit his opponent so hard that he was .... for
   ten minutes.
   a unconscious   b asleep   c knocked about   d stopped
   e ignorant

4 The police, despite very careful .... are still no nearer
   discovering who the murderer is.
   a undertakings   b enquiries   c searches   d surveys
   e investigations

5 Today's football match has been .... because of bad
   weather. They will play next Thursday instead.
   a postponed   b cancelled   c decided   d shot up
   e put away

6 In England, the money you borrow to buy a house from a Building Society is
   called a ....
   a loan   b contract   c mortgage   d search fee
   e deposit

7 During the fight outside the football ground, an eighteen-year-old youth was
   accidentally killed. The person responsible was arrested and charged with
   ....
   a manslaughter   b murder   c mugging   d violence
   e fraud

8 If both parties in the strike cannot agree, then the Government are sometimes
   called in to ....
   a settle   b decide   c choose   d arbitrate
   e compromise

9 The soldiers .... around the square.
   a walked   b strolled   c marched   d limped
   e ran

10 The very idea of my being a thief is quite ....
   a absurd   b dishonest   c futile   d risky
   e sorry

11 James never gives up – he's so ....
   a tiring   b persevering   c persuading   d giving
   e powerful

12 Heavy snow .... the train for several hours.
   a cancelled   b hindered   c delayed   d postponed
   e sent

13 According to the weather ...., there will be snow to-morrow.
   a programme   b information   c forecast   d survey
   e news

14 The next .... of "Dallas" will be shown on BBC 1 next Friday at 9 o'clock.
   a part   b programme   c portion   d episode
   e scrial

15 In the distance, they heard the church clock .... midnight.
   a strike   h hit   c sound   d ring
   e beat

9 Missing words – Education

Put the following words into the correct sentences:

pupils	Primary	time-table	terms
headmistress	headmaster	Secondary	curriculum
Public	syllabus	'Prep'	Comprehensive
State	boarding	compulsory	
subjects	staff	co-educational	

1 Music, English and Mathematics are different sorts of ....
   ....

2 The .... are the teachers working in a school.

3 You must go to school between the ages of 5 and 16. It is ....
   ....

4 The person in charge of a school is called the .... or
   the ....

5 Most children, when they are 11 or 12, go to a ....
   .... school.

6 A school where the .... are made up of both boys
   and girls is called a .... school.

7 In England and Wales, the school year is divided into three ....

8 The .... is everything that is taught in a school, while
   the .... is a plan of what is taught in a particular subject.

9 Education from 5–16 is divided into two levels – ....
   and ....

10 If you want to know which day or time you have a particular lesson, you can
   always look at the ....

11 If you want to send your children to a private school, they can go to a
   .... school when they are 5 or 7, and then to a
   .... school when they are 12 or 13.

12 A .... school is one where pupils live all the time
   and only go home to their families in the holidays.

13 Most children in England and Wales (about 95 % of them) go to ....
   .... schools.

10 Out-of-door objects

Write the number of each drawing next to the correct word.

chimney	3
reservoir	7
shutters	5
signpost	11
fence	2
railings	8
drainpipe	12
well	6
cobweb	10
shed	1
hive	9
pillar box	4

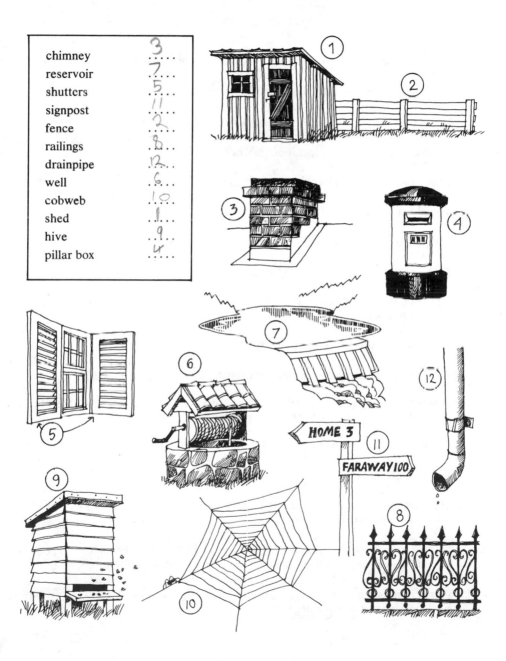

HOME 3

FARAWAY 100

11 Jobs, occupations

Read through the sentences and fill in the missing words.

1 You would go to this person to buy such things as rings, bracelets, watches, etc.

2 His or her job is to arrange dances – especially ballets.

3 This person can help you find a good book to borrow.

4 The doctor who performs operations at a hospital.

5 Agatha Christie made a lot of money because she was this.

6 If your dog dies and you'd like it stuffed, then this is the person to go to.

7 This person writes music for a living.

8 The person who goes with you and looks after you on a package holiday.

9 A man or woman skilled in book-keeping and money matters. They can often help you pay less tax!

10 This person's job is to arrange funerals.

11 This person writes the words for advertisements.

12 This person does all the dangerous acts in films (e.g. jumping off a cliff) so that the actor does not have to take risks. (2 words)

13 His or her job is to study the stars and planets scientifically.

14 The man or woman in charge of a newspaper or magazine.

15 This person is skilled in studying the science of the mind and the way it works so as to affect a person's behaviour.

16 This person's job is to wear new clothes and to show them to people in the hope that they will want to buy them. Usually done by a woman.

17 This person is very good at drawing and designing and usually makes drawings of all the parts of a new building or machine.

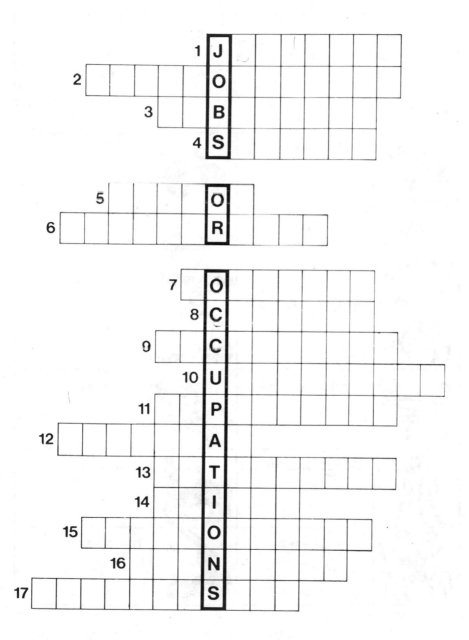

12 Signs of the Zodiac

Write the correct name next to each sign of the Zodiac.

Libra	Pisces	Virgo	Gemini
Taurus	Scorpio	Aries	Aquarius
Leo	Capricorn	Sagittarius	Cancer

	(Jan 20 – Feb 18)		(July 22 – Aug 21)
	(Feb 19 – March 20)		(Aug 22 – Sept 22)
	(March 21 – April 20)		(Sept 23 – Oct 22)
	(April 21 – May 20)		(Oct 23 – Nov 2)
	(May 21 – June 20)		(Nov 23 – Dec 20)
	(June 21 – July 21)		(Dec 21 – Jan 19)

13 Prepositions 1

Put in the missing prepositions in the following sentences:

1 He wasn't short, he wasn't tall; he was .... average height.
   a in   b at   c of   d with

2 "Share this .... yourselves", said the mother to her two children.
   a among   b between   c with   d to

3 What are you going to buy your mother .... her birthday?
   a at   b to   c during   d for

4 The police are looking .... a tall, middle-aged man who was seen stand-
   ing outside the bank just before the robbery took place.
   a after   b for   c to   d with

5 The teacher asked the class to do the exercise .... the bottom of page 7.
   a at   b on   c in   d to

6 As a child I was always ashamed .... my parents because they were
   working-class.
   a with   b over   c by   d of

7 I was always very good .... English when I was at school.
   a in   b at   c with   d on

8 My uncle specializes .... Ancient Greek history.
   a of   b on   c in   d with

9 We arrived .... London at 3.30 in the morning.
   a to   b at   c on   d in

10 Where have you been? I've been waiting .... you for over half an hour!
   a to   b on   c for   d after

11 I didn't see you .... the party last weekend.
   a on   b by   c to   d at

12 There was a lot of coughing .... the performance of Beethoven's Fifth
   symphony.
   a during   b in   c under   d with

14 Phrasal verbs 1

Replace the words in brackets in the following sentences with a suitable phrasal verb. (Make any other necessary changes).

go for	turn up	look after
take after	hold up	go in for
look into	go off	try out
run out of	get over	do away with
call off	go along with	come up with

1 The trouble with Frank is that he never .... on time
  (arrives)
  for meetings.

2 Johnson, I'd like you to .... this complaint we re-
  (examine)
  ceived this morning.

3 The bomb .... with a loud bang which could be
  (exploded)
  heard all over the town.

4 He was walking through the park when a strange dog suddenly ....
  (attacked)
  .... him.

5 I won't be a minute, Jan. I just want to .... my new
  (test)
  tape recorder.

6 You can't have a sandwich, I'm afraid. We've ....
  (used up our supply of)
  bread.

7 Yes, I'll .... that.
  (accept)

8 Because of a heavy downpour, the proposed open-air concert had to be

....
(cancelled)

9 Why don't you .... the "Miss United Kingdom"
                    (enter)
contest, Ulla? I'm sure you'd win it.

10 John, would you .... my handbag while I go to the
                    (take care of)
toilet?

11 I wonder who first .... the idea of wearing seatbelts in
                    (thought of)
cars?

12 What a lovely baby. He certainly .... his father,
                                (resembles)
doesn't he?

13 My father still hasn't really .... the death of my
                                (recovered from)
mother.

14 Because of an accident on the line between Brighton and Victoria, my train was
.... for several hours.
(delayed)

15 I've been feeling so depressed lately that I feel tempted to ....
                                                    (kill)
myself.

23

15 Word building 2

The word in capitals at the end of each of the following sentences can be used to form a word that fits suitably in the blank space. Fill each blank in this way.

Example: During the War there was a great ..*SHORTAGE*..   SHORT
         of sugar, coffee and other goods.

1 There was a lot of .... this morning   ACTIVE
   as work began on the new supermarket.

2 I can think of .... reasons for not   COUNT
   getting married; but even so, I still want to one day.

3 The lovers stood, hand in hand, gazing at the ....   STAR
   sky.

4 As the child's head went under the water for the third   POWER
   time, I stood and watched – .... to
   help. I couldn't swim.

5 I'd love to come to your party but, ...,   FORTUNE
   I have to go somewhere else.

6 Thousands of people turned up for the Pop Festival where   ATTRACT
   the big .... was Bob Dylan.

7 I'm afraid you'll have to see Mr Pound. All matters con-   RESPONSE
   cerning finance are his ....

8 It is ....to take credit for other people's   MORAL
   ideas.

9 Some people claim to be able to ....   TELL
   the future.

10 I hope there won't be too much ....   DIFFICULT
   in getting a work permit.

11 How are you getting on with your ....   CORRESPOND
   course in Russian?

12 What time do you .... start work?   USE

13 There was ice on the pavement which made it very diffi-   SLIP
   cult to walk as it was so ....

14 I could never be a teacher. I'm far too ....   PATIENT

15 I don't know what's the matter with Tommy lately. His   BEHAVE
.... seems to be getting worse and
worse.

16 No matter how much people would wish it, it is very   EQUAL
doubtful whether there will ever be true ....
between the sexes.

17 Most of the .... in this morning's   HEAD
newspapers were about the plane crash between Malmö
and Copenhagen.

18 What .... do you need to become a   QUALIFY
doctor?

19 The sudden .... of one of the   APPEAR
cashiers shortly after the bank robbery confirmed the
police's suspicions that it had been an inside job.

20 The morning following the showing of a documentary   COMPLAIN
about homosexuality, the BBC Television Centre was
flooded with .... from angry viewers.

16 The body – Internal organs

Write the number of each drawing next to the correct word.

diaphragm	. . . . .
gall bladder	. . . . .
rectum	. . . . .
intestines (bowels)	. . . . .
bladder	. . . . .
windpipe (trachea)	. . . . .
gullet (esophagus)	. . . . .
liver	. . . . .
heart	. . . . .
lungs	. . . . .
kidneys	. . . . .
stomach	. . . . .

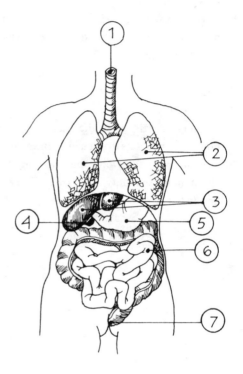

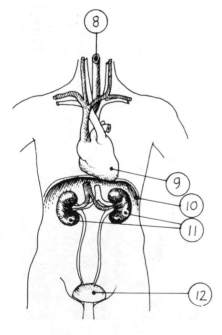

17 Words beginning with "In"

Read through the sentences and fill in the missing words, all of which begin with "in-".

#	Clue	Grid
1	To breathe in.	I N _ L _
2	Without life, not living.	I N _ _ M
3	Synonym for wrong.	I N _ R
4	The opposite of superior.	I N _ _ I
5	You need these before you start to make a cake.	I N _ E _ N _
6	The opposite of guilty.	I N _ _ E
7	A person who is ill or weak through illness or injury.	I N _ L
8	To make up or produce for the first time (e.g. dynamite).	I N _ N
9	A beetle is one of these.	I N E
10	Too quiet to be heard.	I N _ D _ _
11	A measurement.	I N
12	To blow up (e.g. a balloon).	I N _ A _
13	The money you get as payment for work.	I N _ M
14	Synonym for unbelievable.	I N _ _ D _ L
15	Too strong to be destroyed.	I N _ S _ _ _ T _ _ _
16	Synonym for to show.	I N _ I
17	Synonym for hard-working.	I N _ _ T _ U _
18	A young child.	I N _ N
19	To give knowledge or information to someone.	I N _ R _
20	You must have this if you have a car in case you are ever involved in an accident.	I N _ _ A _ _

18 Indoor objects and things

Write the number of each drawing next to the correct word or words.

pane	2
sponge	7
whisk	4
frame	3
spin dryer	1
towel	6
tablecloth	11
magnifying glass	10
sheet	9
cot	12
laundry-basket	5
quilt	8

19 Choose the word 2

Choose the word which best completes each sentence.

1 He lived on the .... of the city.
   a boundary   b suburbs   c outside   outcast
   e outskirts

2 The .... in the south of Sweden is very rich and fertile.
   a ground   b soil   c earth   d land
   e marsh

3 She never really .... her parents for not having allowed her to go to
   university.
   a excused   b pardoned   c forgot   d forgave
   e acquitted

4 When I inherited my grandmother's cottage in Wales, since I didn't need to live
   in it myself, I .... it to an old couple in the village for only
   £5 a week.
   a hired   b rented   c let   d lent
   e leased

5 How much does he .... for cleaning windows?
   a cost   b charge   c demand   d need
   e ask

6 I don't know if you've heard, but there's a .... going
   around the office that Mr Fletcher is leaving at the end of the month.
   a rumour   b reputation   c news   d saying
   e report

7 Mr Goodchild is honest; and I mean "honest" in the broadest ....
   of the word.
   a meaning   b value   c point   d idea
   e sense

→

8 If .... prices go on increasing as they have done for the past few months, then the Government will have to step in and impose some sort of price freeze.

   a   actual   b   current   c   ready   d   monetary
   e   topical

9 My husband often does .... with people from Japan.

   a   business   b   finances   c   affairs   d   concerns
   e   economy

10 Why don't you become a teacher? There's a great .... of them at the moment.

   a   shortage   b   need   c   requirement   d   want
   e   loss

11 Have you written off to the College for a copy of their .... yet?

   a   programme   b   catalogue   c   pamphlet   d   literature
   e   prospectus

12 Did you watch the football .... between Sweden and Denmark on television last night?

   a   play   b   match   c   game   d   sport
   e   competition

13 Many villagers in Africa still make boats out of tree ....

   a   roots   b   branches   c   stems   d   trunks
   e   petals

14 These jeans are terrible. Look how much they've .... since I washed them. They're much too small to wear now.

   a   narrowed   b   lessened   c   shrunk   d   shortened
   e   creased

15 Washing-up has become so much easier since we bought a ....

   a   washing machine   b   dish machine   c   disher   d   plate rack
   e   dishwasher

20 Definitions 2 – "Parts of the body" expressions

Fill in the missing words in the sentences below. Choose from the following:

a brainwave	all fingers and thumbs	down in the mouth
cheeky	to put one's foot in it	to stick one's neck out
wet behind the ears	hair-raising	heartless
an eyesore	off one's head	nosy
to see eye to eye with someone	to show a leg	a pain in the neck

1 .... is something (often a building) which is ugly to look at.

2 .... means to say the wrong thing or to make an awkward mistake.

3 To be .... means to be depressed.

4 Someone who is .... is a very irritating, tiresome person.

5 If you are ...., it means you are cruel.

6 To be .... means to be mad or crazy.

7 .... is a sudden, clever idea.

8 A person who is .... is very inquisitive – especially about things which are none of his or her business.

9 .... means to agree.

10 .... means to take a risk.

11 A .... person is someone who is rude or impolite.

12 If something is ...., then it is frightening.

13 If you are ...., you are young and inexperienced.

14 A person who is .... is a clumsy person.

15 .... means to get out of bed.

21 What is it part of?

Complete the following sentences by choosing an appropriate word from the ones on the right. Look at the example first.

1	A stem is part of	*a flower*	a car
2	A trunk is part of	*a car*	a jug
3	A rung is part of		a nut
4	A hand is part of		a comb
5	A spoke is part of		a ladder
6	A chassis is part of		a shoe
7	A trigger is part of		an apple
8	A core is part of		a flower
9	A cuff is part of		a book
10	A kernel is part of		a gun
11	A yolk is part of		a fountain pen
12	A bridge is part of		a clock
13	A handle is part of		a violin
14	A lens is part of		a wheel
15	A leg is part of		a candle
16	A wick is part of		a tree
17	A nib is part of		a camera
18	A heel is part of		an egg
19	A tooth is part of		a chair
20	A jacket is part of		a shirt

22 Insects

Write the number of each drawing next to the correct word.

fly	13
mosquito	14
butterfly	2
moth	9
bee	7
wasp	12
ant	8
grasshopper	6
ladybird	11
beetle	4
dragonfly	1
spider	10
cricket	5
caterpillar	3

23 Phrasal verbs 2

Replace the words in brackets in the following sentences with a suitable phrasal verb. (Make any other necessary changes).

clear up	go down with	fall off
come into	bring out	fall through
come up against	look up to	look back on
butt in	cut down on	call for
grow out of	come across	break down

1 I do wish you wouldn't ...., Charles. I'm trying to
                   (interrupt)
  talk to your father.

2 When my grandmother died, I .... quite a lot of
                   (inherited)
  money.

3 The only teacher I ever .... at school was Mr White-
               (admired)
  side, the English master.

4 We'll have to get Anne some new clothes soon. She's ....
                              (become too big for)
  the ones she's got.

5 It was while I was clearing out the attic that I ....
                            (found by accident)
  some old photographs of my sister's wedding.

6 I had never .... the problems of loneliness and
             (been faced with)
  isolation until I came to Sweden.

7 Although the attendance was excellent at the start of the season, Chelsea played so badly that, by January, the attendance had ....
(decreased)
by as much as 50 %.

8 I see they're going to .... a book of Peter's poems
(publish)
in the autumn.

9 They were planning to hold a Pop Concert in one of the parks but it ....
(failed to
.... owing to opposition from the local residents.
materialize)

10 I've tried to .... the number of cigarettes I smoke
(reduce)
but it's far too difficult, I'm afraid.

11 When I'm eighty, I'll probably .... my life and
(remember)
realise what a mess I made of it.

12 I do hope it .... soon. Otherwise, we won't be able
(becomes fine)
to have our picnic.

13 I wonder if you could .... me on your way to the
(collect)
party?

14 I'm afraid Paul can't come with us after all – he's just ....
(become ill with)
flu.

15 I'm sorry I'm late, but my car .... on the way here,
(stopped working)
so I had to phone for a taxi.

Write one name for each of the following groups. Before starting, look at the example.

1 New York, Paris, London, Oslo
2 whale, bear, hedgehog, chimpanzee
3 beautiful, exciting, fat, heavy
4 poker, chess, dominoes, Mah-jong
5 Australia, Asia, Africa, Europe
6 cellar, kitchen, lounge, parlour
7 chicken, turkey, duck, goose
8 biro, writing paper, ink, pencil
9 slip, panties, petticoat, bra
10 lipstick, mascara, eye-liner, rouge
11 duffel bag, haversack, suitcase, briefcase
12 Atlantic, Pacific, Arctic, Indian
13 oil tanker, schooner, liner, trawler
14 azure, violet, indigo, orange
15 F, P, R, W
16 microscope, compass, sextant, spectro-scope
17 law, medicine, teaching, the church
18 glider, airliner, helicopter, balloon
19 Polynesian, Papuan, Indian, Nordic
20 penicillin, morphine, quinine, codeine

25 Shapes

Write the number of each drawing next to the correct word or words.

triangle	..4..
cross	..1..
pyramid	.11.
square	..9..
rectangle	..8.
circle	.13.
cube	..2..
sphere	.....
cylinder	.....
cone	..6..
quadratic prism	.....
rhombus	.3...
triangular prism	.....

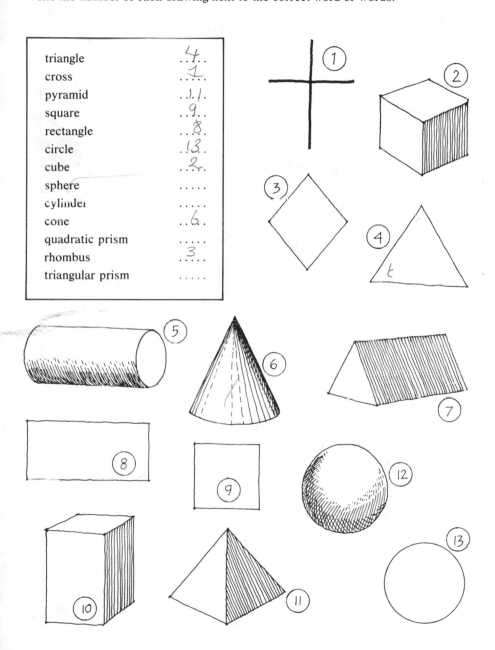

26 Puzzle it out 1 – Which building is which?

Read through the sentences below, then see if you can work out which building is which.

The travel agent's and the supermarket are on the left.

The police station is opposite the supermaket.

The restaurant has a flat roof.

The library is on the same side as the bank.

There's a car parked outside the grocer's.

The cinema is next to the restaurant.

The supermarket has a black roof.

The man has just crossed the road after posting a letter.

Number 1 is the .... Number 5 is the ....

Number 2 is the .... Number 6 is the ....

Number 3 is the .... Number 7 is the ....

Number 4 is the .... Number 8 is the ....

27 Word building 3

The word in capitals at the end of each of the following sentences can be used to form a word that fits suitably in the blank space. Fill each blank in this way.

Example: During the War, there was a great ..*SHORTAGE*..   SHORT
         of sugar, coffee and other goods.

1 The American War of...was   DEPEND
   won in 1776.

2 I was not really surprised that he became a successful   ABLE
   writer because even as a child he showed remarkable
   .... in that direction, writing short
   stories almost as soon as he had learned to read and write.

3 The price of the book is £10, including ....   POST
   and packing.

4 In Sweden, it is customary at a dinner party for the person   SPEAK
   sitting on the left of the hostess to make a ....

5 In my opinion, a large number of parents are quite   FIT
   .... to bring up children.

6 He was not a particularly good teacher, but his students   PERSON
   loved him because he had such a lively ....

7 Parents who smoke .... their chil-   COURAGE
   dren to do likewise, whether they realize it or not.

8 John's beginning to grow out of his jeans. I'd better   LONG
   .... them for him this weekend.

9 It was extremely .... of you to   CARE
   leave your library books on the bus.

10 Although pubs usually close between 10.30 and 11 p.m.,   EXTEND
   they are usually granted an .... until midnight on New Year's Eve.

11 Although the police suspected him of the crime, since   PROVE
   they had no definite .... that he
   was involved, they could not arrest him.

12 I spent my .... in the country.   CHILD ➡

13 After hours of going from one hotel to another, we .... found one which was not fully booked.   EVENT

14 The trouble with Mr Brown is that he's so .... One minute he goes mad when you come late; the next he says nothing. You never know where you are!   CONSIST

15 You can't wear those trousers, Sally. They're far too tight. You look .... in them.   RIDICULE

16 While walking in the mountains in North Wales, we came across a .... quarry.   USE

17 I think it's sheer .... to get married in church if you don't believe in God.   HYPOCRITE

18 At the peace talks to discuss the war in South Africa, the British Foreign Minister told the press that everything was being done to put an end to the .... killing that was going on.   SENSE

19 I don't care what you say. I still think it's very .... not to want to get married and have children.   NATURE

20 In my opinion, all .... are equally bad, irrespective of which party they belong to.   POLITICS

28 Bits and pieces 1

Write the number of each drawing next to the correct word or words.

stopwatch ...2...
lapel ......
postmark ..6...
lampshade ..4...
calendar ..11...
carry cot ..12..
lace ...1...
flowerpot ..8..
heel ..10...
safe ..9...
spear ..3...
companion set ..7...

29 Fruit and vegetables

Write the number of each drawing next to the correct word.

chestnuts	...3.
figs	.....
blackcurrants	/5...
asparagus	.....
parsley	.....
prunes	.....
marrow	.....
parsnips	.....
almonds	.....
onions	.....
cauliflower	.....
dates	.....
blackberries	.....
gooseberries	.....
rhubarb	.....
lettuce	.....
chives	.....
peas	.....
leek	.....
peach	.....

43

30 Missing words – Cars and motoring

Put the following words into the correct sentences:

dip your headlights	change gear	lanes	swerve
skid	driving licence	footbrake	flyover
slip road	rush hour	cat's eyes	hard shoulder
traffic jam	M.o.T. certificate	overtake	
dual carriageway	clutch	lay-by	
ignition key	handbrake	accelerator	

1 To start a car you have to turn the .... to the right.

2 The three pedals on the floor of a car are called (from left to right) the ...., the ....and the ....

3 Before you .... you have to push down or depress the clutch.

4 Before pulling away, you must remember to release the ....

5 If you are driving at night you should always .... when you meet an oncoming vehicle so as not to blind the other driver.

6 To .... another car means to drive past it.

7 To .... means to turn the car suddenly to one side – usually to avoid hitting something or someone. To .... on the other hand, means that the car slides sideways out of control – usually because the road is icy or slippery.

8 If you pass a driving test you are issued with a ....

9 When the road is so full of cars that you can only drive slowly or not at all you are stuck in a .... This usually happens during the .... when people are driving to and from work.

10 In Britain, to help you drive at night, there are .... in the middle of the road. These are metal studs which are reflected by a car's headlights.

11 Most motorways are divided into two or three ....
   The area at the side of a motorway where you can stop (e.g. if you have a
   breakdown) is called the ....

12 The road you enter and leave a motorway by is called the ....
   ....

13 A .... is a road which crosses above another road.

14 A .... is a space next to a road where you can park
   your car out of the way of other traffic.

15 A fast road (not a motorway) with two lanes in each direction is called a
   ....

16 An .... is given to cars more than 3 years old to show
   that they have been examined and judged fit to drive.

31 Choose the answer

Choose the correct word for the definitions in 1–10 and the correct definition for the words in 11–20.

1 The back end of a ship is called
   a the mast   b the poop   c the stern   d the deck

2 A sleeping place on a boat or train is called
   a a cabin   b a bunk   c a berth   d a sleeper

3 A man who breaks into houses, shops or flats – especially at night – is called
   a a thief   b a criminal   c a burglar   d a housekeeper

4 A child who hits smaller or weaker children is called
   a an enemy   b a rascal   c a tyrant   d a bully

5 To cook gently in water without boiling is
   a to fry   b to simmer   c to scramble   d to bubble

6 A person who is able to perform card tricks is called
   a a witch   b a gamble   c a troll   d a conjurer

7 A space next to a road where cars, lorries etc. can park out of the way of the traffic is called
   a a bypass   b a lay-by   c a parking lot   d a junction

8 A chemical substance which you put on cuts, etc. to prevent them from developing disease is called
   a antiseptic   b antitoxin   c antidote   d disinfectant

9 A trick played upon a person in order to make others laugh is called
   a a giggle   b a practical joke   c an April fool   d a jest

10 A person who is very tall and thin is called
   a stocky   b plump   c lanky   d skinny

11 A gutter
   a a pipe at the bottom of the roof to collect rainwater   b a type of headwear
   c a person who is not very brave   d a person who is unable to speak clearly

12 Biennial
   a twice a year   b every two years   c every year   d every leap year

13 A metronome
   a   an evil fairy   b   an instrument used by scientists to determine the age
   of meteors   c   a type of chimney   d   an instrument with a
   pendulum which can be altered to give musicians a regular beat at different speeds

14 To relish
   a   to enjoy   b   to live again   c   to release   d   to put a new cover on a book

15 Insomnia
   a   the inability to keep awake   b   the inability to sleep   c   the inability
   to remember things   d   the inability to have children

16 A busker
   a   a street singer   b   slang for bus conductor   c   a type of plant
   d   a man who studies trees and bushes

17 Dusk
   a   very thick layer of dust   b   the time of day when light first appears
   c   a short, informal discussion   d   the time when daylight is fading

18 Blackmail
   a   slang for bills which come through the post   b   getting money from
   someone by threatening to make known some unpleasant facts about the person
   c   money received through the post on which no tax is paid   d   a sea creature
   with eight arms or tentacles

19 A miser
   a   a very unhappy person   b   a person who studies rats, mice and other rodents
   c   a person who loves money so much that he or she stores it and hardly ever
   spends it   d   the smallest bird in Britain

20 A lodger
   a   a person who pays rent to stay in someone's home   b   an account book
   which records the income and expenditure of a company or business
   c   a person who studies and knows a lot about logic   d   a type of wild cat

32 Name the buildings

Read through the sentences and fill in the missing words.

1 A very large house, usually belonging to a wealthy person, often a nobleman.

2 A place you can stay at if you pay a certain amount of money each night.

3 You stay here when you are ill or injured in some way.

4 A small hut used by shepherds in the Alps during the summer.

5 A strongly-built building, used in the past for defence.

6 Where the King or Queen lives.

7 A flat (usually expensive) at the top of a large building.

8 A house on one level.

9 A large, detached house often used for only part of the year – especially the summer – and very popular in places such as the south of France.

10 Where soldiers live.

11 You usually sleep in one of these when you go camping.

12 A small, roughly-built wooden hut.

13 A house made from blocks of ice.

14 Where red Indians used to live.

15 A small house in the wilds for hunters.

33 Missing words – The Language of Business

Put the following words into the correct sentences:

employees	agent	assembly line
market	export	shareholder
Managing Director	shop steward	profit
Research and	quotation	liquidation
Development	consumers	shares
wholesalers		

1 The person in charge of the running of a company is the ....

2 Firms which buy goods from a factory and later sell them again to shops and stores are called ....

3 People who buy the products of a firm, e.g. food, cars, radios, etc. are called ....

4 A person who acts on behalf of a company – usually overseas – is called an ....

5 People who work in a factory are called ....

6 When a manufacturer tells a buyer before a sale what the particular goods are going to cost as well as the delivery details, he is giving him or her a ....

7 A .... is an elected Union representative working in a factory who represents the other Union members there.

8 The .... department is responsible for finding new ideas and processes.

9 A person who invests money in a company usually buys ....
in that company. He or she is called a ....

10 To sell goods to another country is to .... them.

11 Most cars nowadays are made on an ....

12 The geographical area where goods are sold is called the ....

13 If a limited company cannot pay its debts, then it may have to go into
....

14 If a firm's income is greater than its expenditure, it will make a ....

34 Add a letter

Add **one letter** to each of the following words (in any place) to form a new word. A clue is given to help you. Look at the example first.

1	NOW	...*SNOW*...	seen in winter
2	PACE	....	what most people would like to see
3	PURE	....	a container
4	CRATES	....	lots of these on the moon
5	HOST	....	fact or fiction?
6	PINT	....	in England it is considered rude to do this
7	EAR	....	not cheap
8	ROOF	....	you need this to convict someone of a crime
9	PEAR	....	a hunting weapon
10	RAY	....	used for carrying things
11	SWAM	....	a collective term for bees
12	SEW	....	you eat it
13	CRAM	....	made from milk
14	COW	....	a bird
15	SOON	....	a piece of cutlery
16	GRAVE	....	small stones
17	CARS	....	a popular pastime
18	RAT	....	a sort of boat
19	LATE	....	a piece of crockery
20	SAG	....	a difficulty, problem or drawback
21	GEMS	....	they cause disease
22	LANE	....	a tool used by a carpenter
23	BED	....	to curve something
24	LANCE	....	to look quickly
25	LAST	....	smallest in size, amount, etc.

35 Geography

Write the numbers on the following map of the world next to the correct word or words.

Arctic circle	....	Pacific Ocean	....
Equator	....	Tropic of Cancer	....
Atlantic Ocean	....	Prime meridian	....
Tropic of Capricorn	....	Line of latitude	....
Indian Ocean	....	Mediterranean Sea	....
Line of longitude	....	Antarctic circle	....

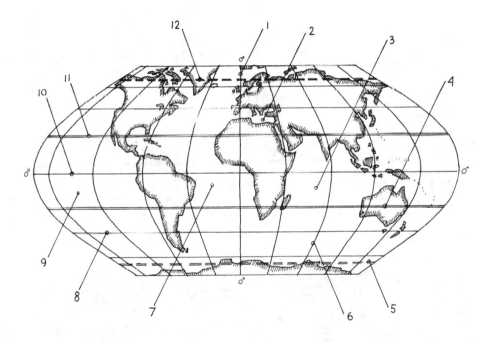

36 Cartoons

In the following cartoons the captions (i.e. the words that go with a cartoon) have got mixed up, so that each cartoon has been printed with the wrong caption under it. Work out the correct caption for each cartoon.

Cartoon		Correct caption	Cartoon		Correct caption
1	–	....	6	–	....
2	–	....	7	–	....
3	–	....	8	–	....
4	–	....	9	–	....
5	–	....	10	–	....

37 Word Association

Each word in the following groups of four words is connected with the same thing. Write down the missing word in each group.

Example: clutch, brake, indicator, wheel = CAR

1 jacket, spine, title, chapter

2 matron, ward, surgeon, theatre

3 vault, deposit, counter, cash

4 receiver, dial, code, exchange

5 javelin, relay, shot, hurdles

6 ribs, neck, string, bow

7 clubs, shuffle, pack, deal

8 aisle, sermon, pew, tower

9 square, root, divide, fraction

10 shelf, reference, book, lend

11 trunk, bark, branch, rings

12 pupil, iris, lash, glasses

13 depression, front, outlook, forecast

14 column, circulation, leader, article

15 pump, saddle, crossbar, spoke

16 frame, canvas, signature, landscape

17 aerial, tube, volume, channel

18 horn, udder, graze, milk

19 crime, bench, magistrate, case

20 stern, rails, funnel, deck

38 Puzzle it out 2: Who won the Cup?

Read through the sentences below, then see if you can fill in the names of the football teams on the chart and thus find out who won the Cup.

Quarter-final	Semi-final	Final
.... **2**		
.... **1** } .... **0** }		
.... **2**		.... **1**
.... **4** } .... **1** }		
.... **1**		
.... **0** } .... **3** }		
.... **2**		.... **3**
.... **3** } .... **2** }		
Winner:		

Arsenal lost by one goal in the semi-final.

Ipswich scored two goals in the quarter-final.

Manchester United beat Leeds.

Aston Villa scored one goal less than the team that beat them in the semi-final.

Tottenham played Arsenal in the quarter-final.

Liverpool beat Cardiff by twice as many goals in the quarter-final.

Leeds lost 0–1 in the quarter-final.

39 Words ending in - o

Read through the sentences and fill in the missing words, each of which ends in "o".

1 The most important character in a play, story, poem, etc.

2 A type of cattle found mainly in Africa and Asia.

3 A sound sent back or repeated, e.g. from inside a cave or an empty room, etc.

4 The inner courtyard of a Spanish house, open to the sky.

5 A blood-sucking insect.

6 Prince Charles's favourite sport.

7 A part of a city where very poor people live or people who are not accepted as full citizens. (e.g. the Jews during World War II.)

8 A type of dance.

9 A place where you can play games (e.g. roulette) for money.

10 An infectious disease which often results in paralysis.

11 To be........................ is to hide your own identity by taking another person's name when your own is well-known.

12 A mountain with a crater at the top out of which lava escapes from time to time with a powerfully explosive force.

13 A musical instrument.

14 A member of a small fighting force specially trained for dangerous enterprises against the enemy.

15 Where an artist or photographer works.

16 The young of any creature in its first state before birth, or before coming out of an egg.

17 The goods carried by ship, plane or other vehicle.

18 The ring of light around a saint's head in a painting.

19 A short sentence or phrase taken as the guiding principle of a person and the way he or she behaves, or of a family or of a school, etc.

20 A type of heel on women's shoes, especially popular during the 60s.

#							
1							O
2				F			O
3							O
4					A		O
5				Q			O
6							O
7					E		O
8						N	O
9					S		O
10						L	O
11		N			N		O
12				L			O
13					I		O
14				M			O
15				T			O
16				E			O
17						R	O
18							O
19						T	O
20			T				O

40 Phrasal verbs 3

Replace the words in brackets in the following sentences with a suitable phrasal verb. (Make any other necessary changes).

back (someone) up	let (someone) down	hold down
keep up with	give up	do up
look down on	go round	take on
hold on	go through	go around with
break up	turn in	take in

1 Have a piece of chocolate. I think there's enough to ....
(be shared among everyone)

2 The meeting was a very long one and didn't ....
(finish)
until 11.30 p.m.

3 If you're still looking for a job, Fred, I believe Warner & Sons are ....
(employing)
.... new people.

4 I do hope you'll excuse me if I ....now; it's just
(go to bed)
that I have to get up early in the morning.

5 I don't know what's wrong with Joanna's husband. He's been given the sack
again. He just can't seem to ....a job.
(keep)

6 Look, if I tell Mr Blake that we're not prepared to work overtime tonight, will
the rest of you ....?
(support me)

7 You will do it, won't you, Anne? Promise me you won't ....
(disappoint me)

8 I think you'll have to explain it all again, Sam. It was far too complicated to

.... all at once.

(understand)

9 My father has always .... working-class people. It's strange really

                (despised)

when you consider that his own father was a coal miner.

10 Oh, darling, would you .... my buttons, please?

              (fasten)

I've just put nail varnish on and it's still wet.

11 If you'd just .... a moment, Mr Blake, I'll see if Mrs

          (wait)

Wilson is free.

12 Arthur's .... a very strange crowd of people these

         (keeping company with)

days, isn't he?

13 Poor Pam! She's really .... a lot this past year, what

         (suffered)

with the death of her mother, her divorce and now losing her job. I feel really

sorry for her.

14 He had to work very hard to .... the others in the

         (maintain the same standard as)

class.

15 It's easy to .... smoking. I've done it lots of times!

      (stop)

41 British and American English

Write down the British or American words for the following:

AMERICAN ENGLISH	BRITISH ENGLISH
1 eraser	....
2	aerial
3 band-aid	....
4	bill (at a restaurant)
5 bathrobe	....
6	biscuit
7 bureau	....
8	caretaker
9 closet (for hanging clothes)	....
10	curtains
11 freeway	....
12	lorry
13 kerosene	....
14	nappy
15 vest	....

42 Bits and pieces 2

Write the number of each drawing next to the correct word.

acorns	10
staples	2
bolt	11
collar	5
dart	8
greenhouse	1
label	4
mitten	9
rattle	3
skull	12
witch	7
kite	6

43 Prepositions after verbs

Fill in the missing prepositions.

1 The headmaster accused the boy .... stealing.

2 I must apologise .... not replying sooner, but I'm afraid I've been rather busy lately.

3 My parents don't approve .... smoking.

4 Do you believe .... God?

5 I look forward .... seeing you again.

6 Now then, John, remember that I'm relying .... you to see that there's no trouble at the party on Saturday.

7 I get very annoyed .... people who don't queue at bus stops.

8 The piece of paper burst .... flames.

9 The only way to cure someone .... biting their nails is to knock their teeth out!

10 One person I always laugh .... when I see him on television is Dave Allen.

11 I think my girlfriend is getting tired .... me.

12 Who is responsible .... spilling ink over my book?

13 Can you think .... a synonym for "stubborn"?

14 My wife is always complaining .... her boss.

15 My brother once confided .... me the fact that he was in love with someone thirty years older than himself.

16 It amazes me how some women can cope .... both a job and a family.

17 There can't be many people in the world who have never heard .... the Beatles.

18 I object .... the way some people look down on you just because you happen to be a foreigner.

19 The man was arrested and charged .... murder.

20 Although I've tried many times, I've never once succeeded .... giving up smoking for more than a few days.

44 Newspaper Misprints

In each of the following extracts from a newspaper there is a misprint. Underline the word which is wrong and also write down which word should have been used instead. (See example).

1 Lost: black and white <u>kitchen</u>, four months old, Farm Road area.
   (........ *KITTEN* ....)

2 Police say the car was later found abandoned 500 years away in a car park off Bridge Road. (.......................................)

3 Three old men sat on the wench, eating sandwiches. (.......................................)

4 February 18th, at Grove Road, Bristol, to Mr and Mrs Andrew Burgess, a daughter (bath well). (.......................................)

5 The dog was seen swimming around unable to get out of the water. The police were old and they asked the fire brigade for help. (.......................................)

6 He told police officers that he had met a man with a ginger bear in the pub who had offered him £100. (.......................................)

7 Pedigree Alsatian pubs for sale. (.......................................)

8 Infra-red ultra-violent lamp for sale. £50 o.n.o. (.......................................)

9 Enjoy our large airy rooms for small families. Home-type food, diets catered for. Scandinavian pastries, home-made pies, country fresh eggs. Hospital is the aim here. (.......................................)

10 Evening course: Bras rubbing, starts March 17th for 6 weeks.
   (.......................................)

11 Gardener required, part-time, 8 hours per weed. (.......................................)

12 Fifty paperback boots, assorted, £4. (.......................................)

13 Day and night security officers wanted. £80 per week whilst raining.
   (.......................................)

14 Herring aid, behind the ear type. No wires, unused. (.......................................)

15 Sin problems? Also acne. Telephone us for free consultation. (.......................................)

16 We should all take care of our wildlife as, with the treat of a nuclear war hanging over us, we should be happy while we can and try to protect all birds.
   (.......................................)

17 Gardens dug, widows washed, and chimneys swept, in Swansea area.
   (.......................................)

18 Modern, semi-detached resident for sale. £35,000. (.......................................)

19 Forecast: some bright intervals with shattered showers. (.......................................)

20 New bride, complete with bit and reins. (.......................................)

45 Where?

Read through the sentences and fill in the missing words.

1 The place where legal matters are decided.

2 The place where plays and musicals are performed.

3 The place where a town's water supply is stored.

4 The place where young flowers and plants are cultivated.

5 The place in a bank where money and valuables are kept.

6 The place where fish are kept.

7 The place, often in the open, where many different sorts of goods can be bought.

8 The place where wild animals are kept for the public to see.

9 The place where you find other animals such as cows, sheep, chickens, pigs, etc.

10 The place where gas is stored.

11 The place where fruit trees grow.

12 The place in a factory where goods are stored.

13 The place where criminals are kept.

14 The place where they clean clothes, sheets, etc.

15 The place where birds are kept.

16 The place where dead people are buried.

17 The room where doctors receive their patients.

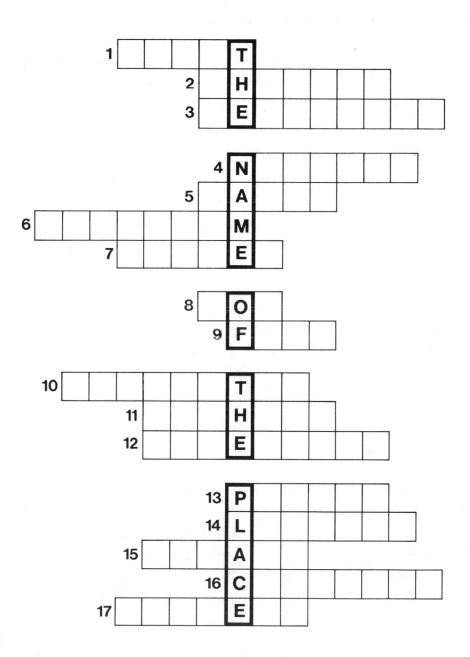

THE NAME OF THE PLACE

46 Missing words – "A scrap of" etc.

Put the following words into the correct sentences:

sip	plate	spoonful
pinch	row	drop
ounce	dab	puff
flight	beam	scrap
bouquet	lock	wisp

1 I wrote his telephone number down on a .... of paper I found in my jacket pocket.

2 See that .... of houses over there? Well, I was born in the end one – number 11.

3 I've never tried whisky before, so do you think I could have a .... of yours, Doreen, just to see if I like it or not?

4 The little girl stepped forward and presented the Lord Mayor with a small .... of flowers.

5 A tiny creature was picked up in the .... of light from my torch. It was a mole.

6 I think we'd better go inside; I just felt a .... of rain.

7 My husband broke his leg when he fell down a .... of stairs at work last summer.

8 I think the painting's quite good, but perhaps it needs just a .... of blue here.

9 Oh, David, I couldn't have a .... of your cigarette, could I?

10 My mother used to keep a .... of my hair in the top drawer of her dressing table.

11 Finally, add a .... of salt. Then, mix the ingredients thoroughly.

12 In the distance we could see the cottage. We knew she was in because a tiny
.... of smoke was coming from her chimney.

13 Does James take one .... of sugar in his coffee or two?

14 I'm sorry, Pam, I can't help any more. I haven't got an .... of energy
left in my body.

15 She put a .... of sandwiches on the table and told them to help them-
selves.

47 Musical instruments

Write the number of each drawing next to the correct word or words.

French horn	.....
flute	.....
trumpet	.....
violin	.....
kettle drum	.....
bassoon	.....
trombone	.....
'cello	.....
bongoes	.....
mouth organ	.....
clarinet	.....
double bass	.....
tuba	.....
oboe	.....
accordion	.....

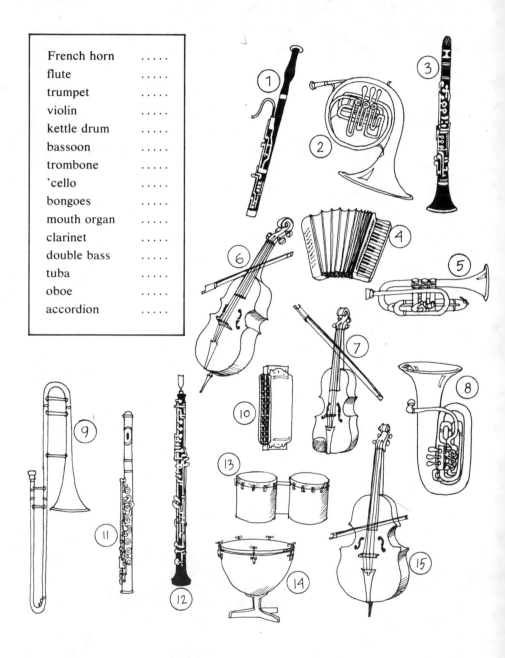

48 Confusing words

Choose the correct word in each of the following sentences.

1 Don't tell my mother that you're having a baby. It's just that since you're not married ... well ... you know how (prudent/prudish) she is. She's bound to be shocked.

2 A (classical/classic) example of actors and actresses playing love scenes actually falling in love was when Richard Burton and Elizabeth Taylor were filming "Anthony and Cleopatra".

3 Many people nowadays are changing from large cars to small ones because they are far more (economic/economical).

4 If you try long enough then you'll (eventually/possibly) succeed.

5 Miss Bright's really (effective/efficient), isn't she? I hate to think what would happen to the office if she ever decided to leave.

6 1066 is one of the most (historical/historic) moments in British history.

7 I can't read David's handwriting at all; it's quite (eligible/illegible).

8 The Centre Party has been (consequential/consistent) in its policy of opposing nuclear power.

9 The new price increases will take (affect/effect) on April 1st.

10 If animals have to be killed for food, then it should be done as (humanly/humanely) as possible so that the animal doesn't suffer needless pain.

11 Did you have (an opportunity/a possibility) to visit the Louvre when you were in Paris?

12 The question of equality between the sexes is very (actual/topical) nowadays.

13 My teacher (complemented/complimented) me on my essay. She said it was the best thing she had read for a long time.

14 What I thought was a genuine Van Gogh turned out to be a forgery. As a result, the painting is now quite (worthless/invaluable).

15 Who else was at the party (beside/besides) the people from the office?

16 I just want to go to the (stationary/stationery) department to buy some envelopes.

17 People who emigrate to a new country usually take a while to (adapt/adopt) to the new way of life.

18 I find it impossible to sleep because of the (continuous/continual) noise from the party in the flat above.

19 Only the most (imminent/eminent) scientists win the Nobel Prize.

20 She started to cry when I told her that her essay was full of mistakes and would have to be rewritten. But it wasn't my (intention/meaning) to upset her; I was trying to be constructive.

49 Choose the word 3

Choose the word which best completes each sentence.

1 I can't read what you've written, I'm afraid. Your handwriting is totally
....

    a messy   b illegible   c illiterate   d spoilt
    e wrong

2 Only three people .... the crash. Everyone else was killed.

    a lived   b recovered   c relieved   d survived
    e overcame

3 I've decided to make a .... across Europe this summer by
car.

    a voyage   b travel   c crossing   d journey
    e package tour

4 Excuse me, Mr Blake, but there's a/an .... message for
you from your wife.

    a vital   b hasty   c urgent   d impotent
    e valuable

5 Is it possible to .... now for next term's evening classes?

    a enlist   b join in   c inscribe   d enrol
    e enter

6 I can't play this afternoon, I'm afraid. I've .... my ankle.

    a turned   b stretched   c pulled   d strained
    e sprained

7 .... he was nearly seventy-five, he could still beat me at
tennis.

    a In spite of   b Since   c Although   d Despite
    e As

8 The trouble with eating oranges is that there are too many
.... inside.

    a pips   b stones   c seeds   d nuts
    e peel

9 It costs £5 a year to .... to this magazine.

    a join   b subscribe   c support   d pay
    e deliver

➡

10 If you take that camera back to England with you, you'll have to pay Customs
.... on it.
   a tax   b expenses   c duty   d prices
   e fines

11 The meeting will begin at 10.30 ....
   a exact   b on time   c sharp   d accurate
   e immediately

12 When I was a child, my parents wouldn't .... me stay out
later than 9 o'clock in the evenings.
   a permit   b allow   c want   d let
   e leave

13 When my father died, I had no .... but to leave school and
get a job.
   a possibility   b choice   c hope   d chance
   e reason

14 He was .... with robbery.
   a charged   b arrested   c held   d imprisoned
   e accused

15 Liberace has a swimming-pool in his garden in the .... of a
piano.
   a form   b design   c figure   d plan
   e shape

50 Definitions 3 – more "Parts of the body" expressions

Fill in the missing words in the sentences below. Choose from the following:

put someone's back up	pull someone's leg	by ear
live from hand to mouth	pay through the nose	pick someone's brains
lose one's head	give someone the cold shoulder	tight-fisted
lose heart	tongue-twister	tongue-tied
Keep your hair on!	be up in arms over/about something	tongue-in-cheek

1 To .... means that you spend all your money as soon as you get it and never save for the future. You just live from day to day.

2 If you play a musical instrument .... , it means you play it without using printed music – you play it from memory.

3 To .... means to become discouraged.

4 To .... means to be very angry or to protest very strongly about something.

5 If a person is ...., he or she is too shy or nervous to speak.

6 To .... means to make someone angry or annoyed.

7 To .... means to panic or lose control of oneself.

8 A .... person is someone who is very mean.

9 To .... means that you ignore him or her and treat him or her in an unfriendly way.

10 If you say to someone "..", you mean "Keep calm!" or "Don't get angry."

11 To .... means to talk to someone about a problem in order to make use of his or her knowledge or ideas.

12 If you .... for something, it means that you give more money for something than it is worth.

13 If you say something ...., it means that your words are not to be taken seriously. (You are saying one thing but often really meaning quite the opposite.)

14 To .... means to tease someone — usually by telling the person something which is quite untrue.

15 A .... is a long word or phrase which is very difficult to say quickly or correctly. (e.g. She sells sea-shells on the sea shore.)

Answers

TEST 1

goblet	4
tea caddy	10
barrel	7
bread bin	2
crate	12
filing cabinet	15
carrier bag	14
sheath	5
satchel	9
cage	1
rucksack	6
keg	3
wastepaper basket	13
litterbin	11
trunk	8

TEST 2

1 (8-e)
2 (9-k)
3 (12-g)
4 (1-c)
5 (6-j)
6 (11-b)
7 (5-l)
8 (2-f)
9 (7-d)
10 (3-h)
11 (10-i)
12 (4-a)

TEST 3

hatchet	2
callipers	6
mallet	12
spirit level	5
hoe	9
tape measure	1
pickaxe	10
oilcan	8
trowel	4

hacksaw	11
awl	7
fork	3

TEST 4

1 headline
2 action replay
3 serial
4 circulation
5 review
6 editor
7 classified
8 article
9 dubbed
10 journalist
11 channels
12 documentary
13 chat show
14 series
15 caption
16 leader
17 cartoon strip
18 cartoonist
19 quiz
20 gossip column

TEST 5

1 occupation
2 suitable
3 invention
4 impossible
5 harmful
6 successful
7 awake
8 performance
9 doubtful
10 terrified
11 signature
12 applications
13 pleasure
14 sensitive
15 increasingly
16 sympathetic
17 daily
18 happiness
19 unattractive
20 ashamed

TEST 6

1 a timid
2 a garrulous
3 a reliable
4 an absent-minded
5 an industrious
6 a tetchy
7 a bossy
8 a stoical
9 a bitchy
10 a gregarious
11 a punctual
12 a bigoted
13 a witty
14 an impulsive
15 a conceited

TEST 7

1 umpire
2 regretted
3 foretold
4 optimistic
5 mortuary (morgue— American English)
6 inaudible
7 congregation
8 stamina
9 ambidextrous
10 insomnia
11 archipelago
12 biography
13 apologised/apologized
14 surgeon
15 hangover
16 bumper
17 ward

18 somehow
19 collided (possibly crashed)
20 nephew

TEST 8

1 (d) congregation
2 (b) mirage
3 (a) unconscious
4 (b) enquiries
5 (a) postponed
6 (c) mortgage
7 (a) manslaughter
8 (d) arbitrate
9 (c) marched
10 (a) absurd
11 (b) persevering
12 (c) delayed
13 (c) forecast
14 (d) episode
15 (a) strike

TEST 9

1 subjects
2 staff
3 compulsory
4 headmaster/headmistress
5 Comprehensive
6 pupils/co-educational
7 terms
8 curriculum/syllabus
9 Primary/Secondary
10 time-table
11 'Prep'/Public
12 boarding
13 State

TEST 10

chimney	3
reservoir	7
shutters	5
signpost	11
fence	2
railings	8
drainpipe	12
well	6
cobweb	10

shed	1
hive	9
pillar box	4

TEST 11

1 jeweller
2 choreographer
3 librarian
4 surgeon
5 author
6 taxidermist
7 composer
8 courier
9 accountant
10 undertaker
11 copywriter
12 stunt man
13 astronomer
14 editor
15 psychologist
16 mannequin
17 draughtsman

TEST 12

Aquarius
Pisces
Aries
Taurus
Gemini
Cancer
Leo
Virgo
Libra
Scorpio
Sagittarius
Capricorn

TEST 13

1 (c) of
2 (b) between ("among"
      if more than
      two people)
3 (d) for
4 (b) for
5 (a) at
6 (d) of

7 (b) at
8 (c) in
9 (d) in
10 (c) for
11 (d) at
12 (a) during

TEST 14

1 turns up
2 look into
3 went off
4 went for
5 try out
6 run out of
7 go along with
8 called off
9 go in for
10 look after
11 came up with
12 takes after
13 got over
14 held up
15 do away with

TEST 15

1 activity
2 countless
3 starry
4 powerless
5 unfortunately
6 attraction
7 responsibility
8 immoral
9 foretell
10 difficulty
11 correspondence
12 usually
13 slippery
14 impatient
15 behaviour
16 equality
17 headlines
18 qualifications
19 disappearance
20 complaints

TEST 16

diaphragm	10
gall bladder	4
rectum	7
intestines (bowels)	6
bladder	12
windpipe (trachea)	1
gullet (esophagus)	8
liver	3
heart	9
lungs	2
kidneys	11
stomach	5

TEST 17

1 inhale
2 inanimate
3 incorrect
4 inferior
5 ingredients
6 innocent
7 invalid
8 invent
9 insect
10 inaudible
11 inch
12 inflate
13 income
14 incredible
15 indestructible
16 indicate
17 industrious
18 infant
19 instruct
20 insurance

TEST 18

pane	2
(window pane/pane of glass)	
sponge	7
whisk	4
frame	3
spin dryer	1
towel	6
tablecloth	11
magnifying glass	10
sheet	9

cot	12
laundry basket	5
quilt	8

TEST 19

1 (e) outskirts
2 (b) soil
3 (d) forgave
4 (c) let
5 (b) charge
6 (a) rumour
7 (e) sense
8 (b) current
9 (a) business
10 (a) shortage
11 (e) prospectus
12 (b) match
13 (d) trunks
14 (c) shrunk
15 (e) dishwasher

TEST 20

1 an eyesore
2 to put one's foot in it
3 down in the mouth
4 a pain in the neck
5 heartless
6 off one's head
7 a brainwave
8 nosy
9 to see eye to eye
with someone
10 to stick one's neck out
11 cheeky
12 hair-raising
13 wet behind the ears
14 all fingers and thumbs
15 to show a leg

TEST 21

1 a stem is part of a flower
2 a trunk is part of a tree
3 a rung is part of a ladder
4 a hand is part of a clock
5 a spoke is part of a wheel
6 a chassis is part of a car
7 a trigger is part of a gun

8 a core is part of an apple
9 a cuff is part of a shirt
10 a kernel is part of a nut
11 a yolk is part of an egg
12 a bridge is part of a violin
13 a handle is part of a jug
14 a lens is part of a camera
15 a leg is part of a chair
16 a wick is part of a candle
17 a nib is part of a fountain pen
18 a heel is part of a shoe
19 a tooth is part of a comb
20 a jacket is part of a book

TEST 22

fly	13
mosquito	5
butterfly	2
moth	9
bee	7
wasp	12
ant	8
grasshopper	6
ladybird	11
beetle	4
dragonfly	1
spider	10
cricket	14
caterpillar	3

TEST 23

1 butt in
2 came into
3 looked up to
4 grown out of
5 came across
6 come up against
7 fallen off
8 bring out
9 fell through
10 cut down on
11 look back on
12 clears up
13 call for
14 gone down with
15 broke down

TEST 24

1 cities
2 mammals
3 adjectives
4 games
5 continents
6 rooms
7 poultry
8 stationery
9 lingerie
10 make-up
11 luggage
12 oceans
13 ships
14 colours
15 letters
16 instruments
17 professions
18 aircraft
19 races
20 drugs

TEST 25

triangle	4
cross	1
pyramid	11
square	9
rectangle	8
circle	13
cube	2
sphere	12
cylinder	5
cone	6
quadratic prism	10
rhombus	3
triangular prism	7

TEST 26

Number 1 is the travel
agent's
Number 2 is the grocer's
Number 3 is the post office
Number 4 is the supermarket
Number 5 is the library
Number 6 is the police
station
Number 7 is the cinema
Number 8 is the restaurant

TEST 27

1 independence
2 ability
3 postage
4 speech
5 unfit
6 personality
7 encourage
8 lengthen
9 careless
10 extension
11 proof
12 childhood
13 eventually
14 inconsistent
15 ridiculous
16 disused
17 hypocrisy
18 senseless
19 unnatural
20 politicians

TEST 28

stopwatch	2
lapel	5
postmark	6
lampshade	4
calendar	11
carry cot	12
lace	1
flowerpot	8
heel	10
safe	9
spear	3
companion set	7

TEST 29

chestnuts	10
figs	8
blackcurrants	17
asparagus	18
parsley	7
prunes	4
marrow	13
parsnips	5
almonds	3

onions	20
cauliflower	16
dates	11
blackberries	15
gooseberries	19
rhubarb	1
lettuce	2
chives	12
peas	14
leek	9
peach	6

TEST 30

1 ignition key
2 clutch/footbrake/accele-
   rator
3 change gear
4 handbrake
5 dip your headlights
6 overtake
7 swerve/skid
8 driving licence
9 traffic jam/rush hour
10 cat's eyes
11 lanes/hard shoulder
12 slip road
13 flyover
14 lay-by
15 dual carriageway
16 M.o.T. certificate

TEST 31

1 the stern
2 a berth
3 a burglar
4 a bully
5 to simmer
6 a conjurer
7 a lay-by
8 antiseptic
9 a practical joke
10 lanky
11 a pipe at the bottom of
   the roof to collect rainwater

12 every two years
13 an instrument with a pendulum, etc.
14 to enjoy
15 the inability to sleep
16 a street singer
17 the time when daylight is fading
18 getting money from someone by threatening, etc.
19 a person who loves money so much that he or she stores it, etc.
20 a person who pays rent to stay in someone's home.

TEST 32

1 mansion
2 hotel
3 hospital
4 chalet
5 castle
6 palace
7 penthouse
8 bungalow
9 villa
10 barracks
11 tent
12 shanty
13 igloo
14 wigwam
15 lodge

TEST 33

1 Managing Director
2 wholesalers
3 consumers
4 agent
5 employees
6 quotation
7 shop steward
8 Research and Development
9 shares/shareholder

10 export
11 assembly line
12 market
13 liquidation
14 profit

TEST 34

1 snow
2 peace
3 purse
4 craters
5 ghost
6 point
7 dear
8 proof
9 spear
10 tray
11 swarm
12 stew
13 cream
14 crow
15 spoon
16 gravel
17 cards
18 raft
19 plate
20 snag
21 germs
22 plane
23 bend
24 glance
25 least

TEST 35

Arctic circle	12
Equator	10
Atlantic Ocean	7
Tropic of Capricorn	4
Indian Ocean	3
Line of Longitude	6
Pacific Ocean	9
Tropic of Cancer	11
Prime meridian	1
Line of latitude	8
Mediterranean Sea	2
Antarctic Circle	5

TEST 36

Cartoon	Correct caption
1	10
2	8
3	9
4	6
5	3
6	2
7	4
8	1
9	7
10	5

TEST 37

1 book
2 hospital
3 bank
4 telephone
5 athletics
6 violin
7 cards
8 church
9 mathematics
10 library
11 tree
12 eye
13 weather
14 newspaper
15 bicycle
16 painting
17 television
18 cow
19 court
20 ship

TEST 38

Quarter-final

Arsenal	2
Tottenham	1
Cardiff	2
Liverpool	4
Manchester Utd.	1
Leeds	0
Ipswich	2
Aston Villa	3

Semi-final

Arsenal	0
Liverpool	1
Manchester Utd.	3
Aston Villa	2

Final

Liverpool	1
Manchester United	3

Winner: Manchester United

TEST 39

1 hero
2 buffalo
3 echo
4 patio
5 mosquito
6 polo
7 ghetto
8 tango
9 casino
10 polio
   (short for poliomyelitis)
11 incognito
12 volcano
13 piano
14 commando
15 studio
16 embryo
17 cargo
18 halo
19 motto
20 stiletto

TEST 40

1 go round
2 break up
3 taking on
4 turn in
5 hold down
6 back me up
7 let me down
8 take in
9 looked down on
10 do up

11 hold on
12 going around with
13 gone through
14 keep up with
15 give up

TEST 41

American English

1 eraser
2 antenna
3 band-aid
4 check
5 bathrobe
6 cookie
7 bureau
8 janitor
9 closet
10 drapes
11 freeway
12 truck
13 kerosene
14 diaper
15 vest

British English

1 rubber
2 aerial
3 elastoplast
4 bill
5 dressing gown
6 biscuit
7 chest of drawers
8 caretaker
9 wardrobe
10 curtains
11 motorway
12 lorry
13 paraffin
14 nappy
15 waistcoat

TEST 42

acorns	10
staples	2
bolt	11
collar	5
dart	8

greenhouse	1
label	4
mitten	9
rattle	3
skull	12
witch	7
kite	6

TEST 43

1 of
2 for
3 of
4 in
5 to
6 on
7 with
8 into
9 of
10 at
11 of
12 for
13 of
14 about
15 in
16 with
17 of
18 to
19 with
20 in

TEST 44

	Misprint	Correct word
1	kitchen	kitten
2	years	yards
3	wench	bench
4	bath	both
5	old	told
6	bear	beard
7	pubs	pups
8	violent	violet
9	Hospital	Hospitality
10	Bras	Brass
11	weed	week
12	boots	books
13	raining	training
14	Herring	Hearing
15	Sin	Skin

16	treat	threat
17	widows	windows
18	resident	residence
19	shattered	scattered
20	bride	bridle

TEST 45

1 court
2 theatre
3 reservoir
4 nursery
5 vault
6 aquarium
7 market
8 zoo
9 farm
10 gasometer
11 orchard
12 warehouse
13 prison
14 laundry
15 aviary
16 cemetery
17 surgery

TEST 46

1 scrap
2 row
3 sip
4 bouquet
5 beam
6 drop
7 flight
8 dab
9 puff
10 lock
11 pinch
12 wisp
13 spoonful
14 ounce
15 plate

TEST 47

French horn	2
flute	11
trumpet	5

violin	7
kettle drum	14
bassoon	1
trombone	9
'cello	6
bongoes	13
mouth organ	10
clarinet	3
double bass	15
tuba	8
oboe	12
accordion	4

TEST 48

1 prudish
2 classic
3 economical
4 eventually
5 efficient
6 historic
7 illegible
8 consistent
9 effect
10 humanely
11 an opportunity
12 topical
13 complimented
14 worthless
15 besides
16 stationery
17 adapt
18 continuous
19 eminent
20 intention

TEST 49

1 (b) illegible
2 (d) survived
3 (d) journey
4 (c) urgent
5 (d) enrol
6 (e) sprained
7 (c) Although
8 (a) pips
9 (b) subscribe
10 (c) duty
11 (c) sharp

12 (d) let
13 (b) choice
14 (a) charged
15 (e) shape

TEST 50

1 live from hand to mouth
2 by ear
3 lose heart
4 be up in arms over/about something
5 tongue-tied
6 put someone's back up
7 lose one's head
8 tight-fisted
9 give someone the cold shoulder
10 Keep your hair on!
11 pick someone's brains
12 pay through the nose
13 tongue-in-cheek
14 pull someone's leg
15 tongue-twister